Hustling and Bustling
BUSES

WHEELS AND AUTOMOBILES

FOX EYE
PUBLISHING

A bus is a large machine on wheels that moves across the ground.

On country lanes, roads and
motorways, buses zoom around.

Buses carry passengers on trips from A to B.

Can you count the buses in this picture?
How many can you see?

Coaches travel long distances.
They move between cities and towns.

The luggage compartment underneath
is where the bags are found.

bus stop

City buses stop at bus stops.
This is where passengers get on and off.

The passengers press a button.
It tells the driver to stop.

handle

Passengers get on through the front door.
They can buy a ticket inside.

ticket

seat

There are handles for standing and rows
of seats on both sides of a central aisle.

top deck

Double-deckers have a top deck.
They have stairs to climb up inside.

The passengers on the top deck
have an exciting ride up high.

tourist

This tour bus has an open top so tourists can sightsee.

A tour by bus can be such fun
for people like you and me.

A minibus carries smaller groups.
It looks a little like a van.

Which bus can carry sports teams to a match?
A little minibus can!

A trolley bus is powered by electric cables overhead.

electric cable

If a trolley bus needs to go off-route it can use its battery instead.

A shuttle bus carries passengers on short trips from A to B.

When you're going to board an airplane,
it's a shuttle bus that you need.

Bustling Words

An **aisle** is an area between seats through which people walk.

Coaches are large vehicles that carry people on long distances.

A **deck** is the surface of a vehicle on which people walk.

Distances are the measurements of length between places.

A **luggage compartment** is part of a bus or coach in which the passengers' bags are kept.

A **machine** helps us to do work.

A **minibus** is a small van with windows.

Motorways are very big roads that cover long distances.

A **shuttlebus** travels short distances between two places. At an airport, a shuttlebus carries passengers across the runway to the airplane.

Sightsee means to travel around seeing interesting things.

A **tour** is a trip taken by someone who explains what you are seeing along the way.

Tourists are people who go on a tour.

A **trolley bus** is a bus that is powered by electricity from electric cables above the road.

First published in 2024 by Fox Eye Publishing
Unit 31, Vulcan House Business Centre,
Vulcan Road, Leicester, LE5 3EF
www.foxeyepublishing.com

Author: Katherine Eason
Art director: Paul Phillips
Cover designer: Emma Bailey
Editor: Jenny Rush

All illustrations by Eszter Szepvolgyi

978-1-80445-336-0

Printed in China